MOVING PICTURES

A LOOK AT DETROIT FROM HIGH ATOP THE PEOPLE MOVER

BY MANNY CRISOSTOMO
WITH AN INTRODUCTION BY JIM FINKELSTEIN

DETROIT FREE PRESS
1987

MOVING PICTURES

A LOOK AT DETROIT FROM HIGH ATOP THE PEOPLE MOVER

Photography: Manny Crisostomo
Design: Randy Miller
Copy editing: Kathleen O'Gorman, Kelly Feusse
Page production: Carol A. Jaszcz
Color printing: Jessica J. Trevino
Publications co-ordinator: Michele Kapecky

PUBLISHED BY THE DETROIT FREE PRESS
DETROIT, MICHIGAN 48231

Manufactured in the United States of America
ISBN 0-937247-02-2
Cataloging in Publication Number: 87-71506

A gifted photographer looks through the lens of his camera and sees things others do not see.

He may see shades or angles of lighting, combinations of colors, elements of background, or sight lines that otherwise would have eluded others. Whatever the ingredients, the result can be a picture whose story, or mood, equals the proverbial 1,000 words. That picture can give us a brand new vantage point from which to view something that may be old and familiar.

In the coming months and years, as we ride the Detroit People Mover, each of us will have a new vantage point from which to view an old and familiar part of Detroit — our downtown.

Manny Crisostomo has looked from that new vantage point with the eye of a gifted photographer. In the months prior to the opening of the People Mover, he spent countless hours on its elevated guideway, looking through his camera and taking the pictures on the following pages.

The results speak for themselves. I find them thought-provoking and inspiring.

This collection of photographs gives us yet another reason to be glad we persevered to complete this project, which will mean so much to the continued development of Detroit as we enter the 21st Century.

Coleman A. Young

COLEMAN A. YOUNG
Mayor

FOOTLOOSE ON · THE PEOPLE MOVER

BY JIM FINKELSTEIN

Have you ever looked into a mirror at the reflection of a familiar room and suddenly not recognized its fondly treasured furnishings?

So it is with the image of Detroit that unfolds before a wayfarer on the city's newest thoroughfare, and as documented so superbly by Manny Crisostomo's photographs: a curving, 2.9-mile pathway that plunges and soars through an old-shoe city and simultaneously laces it together into a new place altogether.

Standing on the shoulders of the blank concrete pillars that march monotonously at ground level, the traveler is set free of the dust and detritus, the ugliness, the walled-off views and the traffic jams as he rides the sky road that always disappears playfully beyond the next corner.

At times the People Mover guideway cruises among back streets and burned-out hulks of buildings, but at its best — where it slinks among its contemporaries on the riverfront — it's the ribbon tied on a breathtaking cityscape out of a futurist's dream.

Buildings show faces never meant, by their architects, to be glimpsed this way. A new kinship embraces like-level structures in the city's midsection: covered bridges spanning buildings, Joe Louis Arena's space-tube walkway, the steel latticework along Washington Blvd., even the Ambassador Bridge far downriver.

The pathway's gentle swell, almost like an ocean wave, carries the pilgrim along, swooping him low in places, sending him skyward in others and nearly depositing him into the laps of third-floor office workers.

The road threads through stations, including a green-glassed portal in the Millender Center, a mezzanine entrance to Trappers Alley and a steamy welcome alongside the power-plant berm at the Renaissance Center.

Twice the guideway aims directly toward the city's massed skyline at its most impressive: as it banks left around Cobo Hall before heading north and as it emerges on a straightaway at the Kern Block, facing west.

Along the route, buildings stand in new relation above and below. Traversing Larned Street, five towers — the Pontchartrain Hotel, the Buhl Building, the Guardian Building, the Comerica Bank Building and the American Natural Resources Building — close themselves around the traveler, a cloak of steel, glass and stone. At other points, buildings are somehow diminished by the vantage: Those along Greektown's Monroe Street look sad and small.

And the streets below — what becomes of them? The scene looks cleaner, more sophisticated, somehow more appealing. Parks and trees seem vivid and inviting; filled-up parking lots look like festive urban ground covers. Pedestrian and auto traffic hurtles in a more purposeful way, as if toward pressing appointments.

A new sense of internal logic seems to govern a city battered and scattered by time. Riverfront and Grand Circus Park and the banking district are knitted together along this floating highway, which simultaneously lends certitude to the space-age credentials of the Renaissance Center, the Dodge Fountain and the Millender Center skyways.

The circuit runs the gamut from a high-soaring transit of the riverfront to a dodging sneak among Bagley Avenue's low buildings. At times, the traveler can glimpse the route ahead: Crossing the Lodge Freeway at the entrance to Cobo Hall, he looks east to spy the guideway doubling back across Jefferson at the Renaissance Center.

Even from these altitudes, subtle changes emerge in the cityscape. Sighted as the guideway streaks past the Renaissance Center, the far-off concrete blocks of the Frank Murphy Hall of Justice and the Baird Detention Center look to be improbable robotic contraptions. The twin spires of St. Marys Church in Greektown, from this lookout, are salt and pepper shakers.

Buildings are examined with their hemlines slightly raised. The Manufacturers Bank Building on W. Lafayette presents a long portico that seems oddly like a front porch, welcoming guideway-goers. An awning on the Hudson's Building bares an intricate wonder of green-painted wrought iron. Third-floor parking decks leap to prominence.

The apparatus of urban life that once hung unnoticed overhead takes on new immediacy. Neon signs from the city's heyday — "Tuller Parking," "United Artists" — wink like reminders from bygone eras; billboards and marquees now speak directly to the passerby.

Surprises await in unlikely places. Wayne County Community College is a gray wedge of cheese; the Riverfront Apartments towers are keyboards on their sides; the Joe Louis Arena is a gray and orange mass, bristling with tunnels and turrets, and the Cobo Arena parking ramp is an oversized corkscrew.

Irony, too, lies just ahead. Having digested the moonscape, the traveler progresses a few more yards and buildings part to reveal a hazy, distant scene of trees and grass from the world before People Movers — across the river along Windsor's waterfront.

Sights both inspiring and amusing waylay the traveler. Between Hudson's and the Detroit Public Library branch, this legend etched across the library's portal now jumps out at eye level: "Civilization Is the Accumulated Culture of Mankind." At Macomb Street, a row of colorfully painted men — part of an advertisement painted high on the side of a building — stroll alongside the

guideway as if escorting the traveler.

There's a good and a bad side to the city, even from up here. The fun is to be had as the guideway sweeps down Cass with its busy streets, out over the Cobo Hall expansion project, low past Joe Louis Arena and high over the Detroit River. Picture-book views of the riverfront promenade from Cobo to Hart Plaza and of downtown buildings continue as the guideway sweeps right on Larned (with the Veterans Memorial Building's eagle perched reassuringly to the south) and then skids past the Millender and Renaissance centers.

But on the back leg, the guideway passes the shopworn Broadway-Randolph district and the burned and broken theaters ringing Grand Circus Park. In places, the thoroughfare adds nothing to the total but another lump of gray concrete.

Home base is the Maintenance and Control Facility, just north of Michigan Avenue near Cass. Here, the traveler can filter his new vision of the city through yet more glass.

Standing in the adjoining Times Square station, he can wait for the cars arriving on computerized cue in groups of one and two. And he can look through the blue plexiglass of a rapid-transit gate that's typical of subway stops throughout the world. But — surprise! — that city down there is Detroit, the City on Wheels.

This new vision of Detroit flows past riders' windows at up to 30 m.p.h. But who'd have thought they'd ever see it?

PICTURES

A Reflection Of A Mover Vehicle Can Be Seen In Glass Panels Of The Blue Cross-Blue Shield Jefferson Building.

Colorful Gents Painted On The Side Of Serman's Clothes On Randolph Accompany Travelers On The Mover As It Heads Toward Hudson's, A Detroit Landmark Now Unoccupied.

A SOLITARY FIGURE CROSSES FROM THE KERN BLOCK IN THE LATE FALL AFTERNOON.

The Towers Of The Riverfront Apartments On The Bank Of The Detroit River Are Seen Through The Window Of The Mover Vehicle.

LOOKING OUT ON BUILDINGS ON RANDOLPH STREET AND THE MILLENDER CENTER PARKING STRUCTURE, THE DOWNTOWN BUS STATION AND THE CADILLAC SQUARE APARTMENTS.

THE NEIGHBORHOOD IS MIRRORED IN THE PANELS OF THE BLUE CROSS-BLUE SHIELD BUILDING AT JEFFERSON AND BEAUBIEN.

THE LATE AFTERNOON SUN CASTS A SHADOW OVER HALF A BLOCK OF CASS AND LAFAYETTE WHILE DOWNTOWN BUILDINGS LOOM IN THE SUNLIGHT.

Downtown Woodward Avenue In The Early Twilight Of A Fall Day.

WORKERS WALK THE GUIDEWAY AS IT CROSSES JEFFERSON WITH A SEA OF BUILDINGS IN THE BACKGROUND.

A FADED SIGN POINTS THE WAY TO A PARKING LOT ON CASS.

A Detroit Police Horse Gets Free Parking At A Lot At Beaubien And Congress While Its Rider Takes A Lunch Break.

GRAND CIRCUS PARK, AFLUTTER IN AUTUMN LEAVES, INVITES THE EYE, AS WELL AS THE VISITOR, TO DAWDLE.

A CONSTRUCTION WORKER CAREFULLY WALKS THE STEEL BEAMS DURING CONSTRUCTION OF THE COBO HALL EXPANSION PROJECT.

THE AFTERNOON SUN CASTS A SHADOW ON A CONSTRUCTION WORKER PUTTING UP A NEW FENCE ON CONGRESS.

A LONE FIGURE WALKS AMONG THE LONG SHADOWS THAT FILL THE INTERSECTION OF LARNED AVENUE AND WASHINGTON BOULEVARD.

RIDERS FILL THE SEATS AND LOOK OUT THE WINDOWS OF A TROLLEY CAR ON ITS WAY TO HART PLAZA.

People Wait In Line For A Bus Outside The Downtown Library

On Library Avenue.

A PASSERBY CASTS REFLECTIONS ON THE DETROIT FEDERAL SAVINGS BUILDING ON WOODWARD AND LARNED.

A Lone Pedestrian Stands On The Sidewalk Near

Griswold And Larned.

THE MOVER GUIDEWAY ON THE DETROIT RIVER, WITH THE AMBASSADOR BRIDGE AND DOWNRIVER INDUSTRIES IN THE BACKGROUND.

The Skywalk Leads To The Graphic Lines Of The Modernistic Omni International Hotel At The Millender Center.

Pigeons Rest On The Lower Railing On The Back Side Of The Murphy Building On Congress.

LORETTA ANDERSON ENJOYS THE SUMMER SUN FROM ONE OF THE OPEN WINDOWS OF THE AAA MICHIGAN OFFICES ON BAGLEY.

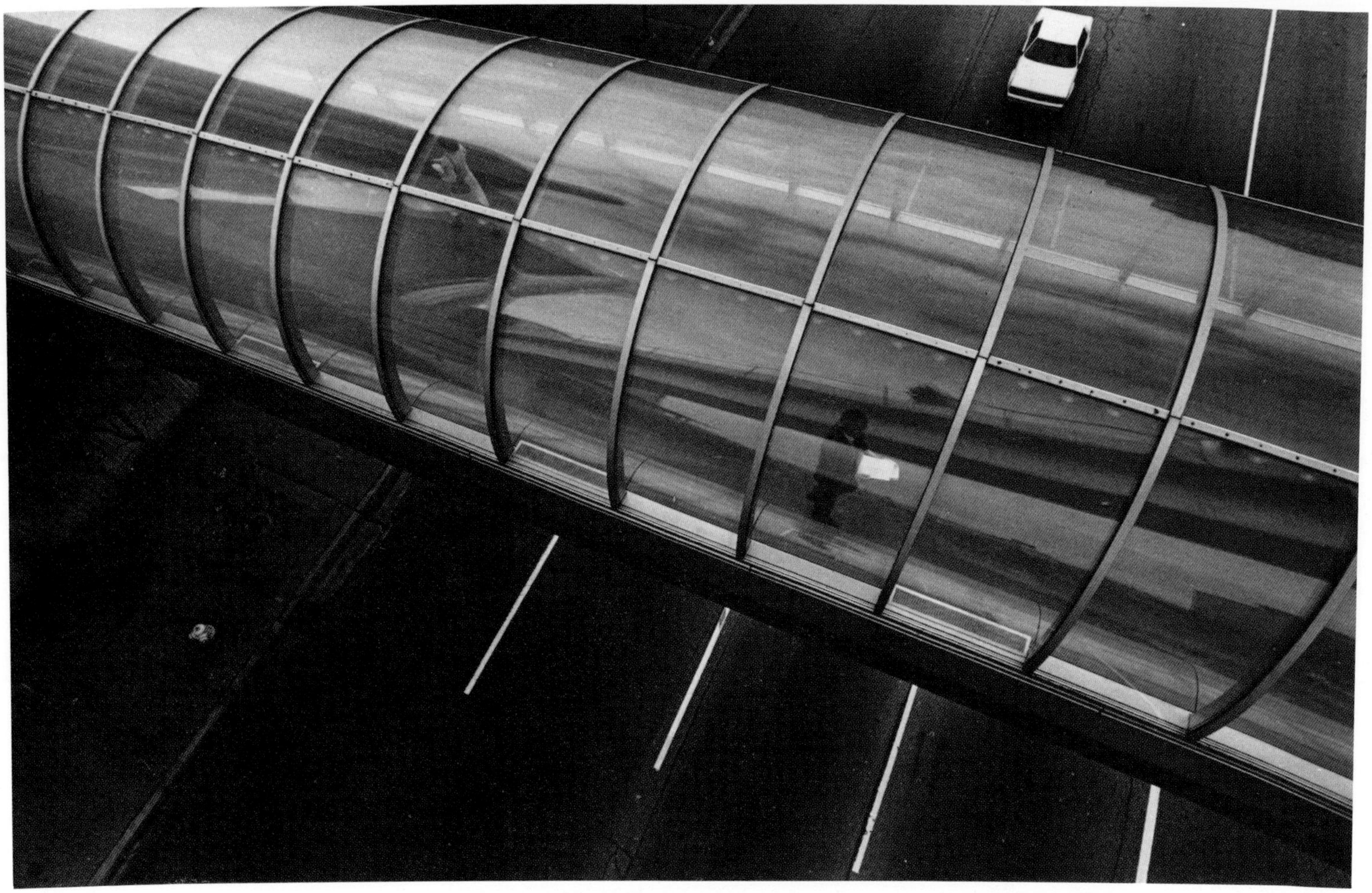

THE SKYWALK FROM THE OMNI INTERNATIONAL HOTEL, ABOVE, SLICES ACROSS JEFFERSON AVENUE TO THE RENAISSANCE CENTER.

LOOKING OUT THE BACK WINDOW OF THE MOVER VEHICLE ONTO THE TRACK THAT LEADS FROM THE RENAISSANCE CENTER.

RIT
THE
Y."
3:17

City-County Building Workers Head Home Under The Watch Of The Spirit Of Detroit Statue.

THE CITY AGLOW WITH CHRISTMAS LIGHTS AND THE AFTERNOON RUSH HOUR ON JEFFERSON AVENUE.

A CONSTRUCTION WORKER SCRAMBLES TO A PRECARIOUS SPOT ON TOP OF A FOUNDATION PILLAR AT THE COBO HALL EXPANSION.

A Crane Operator Works On A Cold Winter Day On The Cobo Hall Expansion.

EARLY EVENING IN GREEKTOWN.

THE TRACK LEADS TO THE DETROIT SKYLINE ON THE GUIDEWAY

BETWEEN COBO AND JOE LOUIS ARENA.

BOBLO BOATS, THE STE. CLAIRE AND THE COLUMBIA, ARE MOTHBALLED FOR THE WINTER AT THEIR DETROIT RIVER MOORING. THE BOATS HAVE SINCE MOVED TO THEIR NEW DOCK AT THE FOOT OF CLARK AVENUE NEAR THE DETROIT MARINE TERMINAL, DOWNRIVER FROM THE AMBASSADOR BRIDGE.

LOOKING INTO THE REFERENCE ROOM OF THE DOWNTOWN LIBRARY. THE WRITING ON THE WALL SAYS "CIVILIZATION IS THE ACCUMULATED CULTURE OF MANKIND."

A CHRISTMAS TREE AND A WREATH ON JEFFERSON AVENUE WITH THE RENAISSANCE CENTER IN THE BACKGROUND.

THE CANADIAN CLUB SIGN IN WINDSOR REFLECTS OFF THE DETROIT RIVER.

THE TROLLEY MAKES ITS WAY ON TRACKS THAT RUN PARALLEL WITH JEFFERSON AVENUE.

A WINTRY SCENE ALONG THE TROLLEY TRACKS NEAR HART PLAZA.

THE STAIRS ZIGZAG UP TO JOE LOUIS ARENA.

TIP TOP
BOOK STORE
OF TITLES
CINE X
Detroit's Most Intimate
Adult Movie Theatre
LEE'S

THE OLD BUILDINGS THAT LINE MONROE SEEM LOST IN A TIME WARP. THE BUILDINGS ARE PART OF THE MONROE BLOCK RESTORATION.

The Balconies Of The Millender Center Apartments, One Of The Renaissance Center Towers And The Statues Wrapped In Plastic On The Old County Building Form An Architectural Composition.

THE TRACK CURVES RIGHT TOWARD THE CADILLAC CENTER PEOPLE MOVER STATION AS THE DOWNTOWN SKYSCRAPERS LOOM IN THE BACKGROUND.

DIRECTLY BELOW THE MOVER ARE SLICES OF CITY LIFE DURING THE FIRST WEEKS OF SPRING, AS A MAN WALKS WITH A BOUQUET OF FLOWERS.

A Busy Lunch-Hour Scene On The Sidewalk At Woodward And Congress.

A Flower Salesman Tends To His Customers At The Larned Entrance Of The City-County Building.

Dining At Open Windows At Niki's Taverna In The Greektown Area On A Warm Spring Day.

"CASS" KEEPS WATCH OVER HER MASTER'S PARKING LOT AT BEAUBIEN AND CONGRESS. THE DOG IS THERE EVERY DAY EXCEPT WEEKENDS.

PEDESTRIANS AND THE TROLLEY SHARE THE SIDEWALK ALONG COBO HALL AND HART PLAZA.

LOOKING STRAIGHT DOWN FROM THE GUIDEWAY ONTO CONSTRUCTION WORKERS ON THE COBO HALL EXPANSION.

A FALL LATE AFTERNOON WALK ON GRATIOT AVENUE

AND FARMER STREET.

Horse And Rider And Motorcyclist Await The Green Traffic Light At The Intersection Of Monroe And Beaubien. The Mounted Officer Works The Greektown Beat.

YAMAHA

A PASSERBY WALKS PAST A ROW OF POSTERS OF MAO TSE-TUNG ON THE UNOCCUPIED METROPOLITAN BUILDING ON JOHN R.

ONE WAY

PEDESTRIANS AND TRAFFIC SIGNS SHARE A STREET SCENE

ON JEFFERSON.

WORKERS LEAVE THE CITY-COUNTY BUILDING ON THE WOODWARD SIDE.

DISCHARGE
ONLY

A WOMAN WAITS FOR A BUS IN FRONT OF THE OMNI INTERNATIONAL HOTEL ON JEFFERSON.

A PARISIAN-LOOKING SCENE OF A WOMAN WALKING AMONG THE PIGEONS AND FALLEN LEAVES OF GRAND CIRCUS PARK.

THE LODGE FREEWAY SCOOTS UNDER THE PEOPLE MOVER AND THE WALKWAY FROM JOE LOUIS ARENA TO THE PARKING GARAGE.

A PEDESTRIAN SCURRIES ALONG A SIDEWALK IN SNOW-COVERED TIMES SQUARE PARK.

THE TREES BLOOM IN GRAND CIRCUS PARK AFTER A WINTER IN THE CITY. THE BUILDINGS ON ADAMS LOOK OVER THE PARK.

AN OLD BILLBOARD STILL TOUTS JILL'S FROSTYLAND, WHICH ISN'T ON E. GRAND RIVER ANYMORE.

THE SPIRAL DRIVEWAY TO THE ROOFTOP PARKING OF COBO HALL ADDS

A CURVING DIMENSION TO THE CITY SKYLINE.

Pedestrians Are Like Chess Pieces In This Checkered Sidewalk In Front Of Manufacturers Bank On W. Lafayette.

Looking Out The Window Of The Vehicle Onto A Piano-Key Design From The American Natural Resources Building On Jefferson.

FAMILY MEMBERS STROLL WITH THEIR SHADOWS ALONG ATWATER STREET AND THE JOE LOUIS ARENA.

A CHILD FROLICS WHILE FOLLOWING HER MOTHER ON AN EMPTY PARKING LOT AT BAGLEY AND CASS.

A FREIGHTER SHARES THE DETROIT RIVER WITH A SMALL BOAT WITH WINDSOR IN THE BACKGROUND.

THE LEAVES CHANGE COLORS IN FRONT OF HART PLAZA AS THE WINDSOR SKYLINE LOOMS ACROSS THE RIVER.

BARBER PETE KITHAS TAKES A BREAK AT PETE'S BARBER SHOP ON MACOMB. PETE HAS BEEN CUTTING HAIR AT THE SAME SHOP FOR 25 YEARS.

SEAMSTRESSES HUDA DABABNEH AND MARY GLODOWSKI (LEFT) AT KAY'S BRIDAL ON BROADWAY LOOK OUT OF WEATHERED WINDOWS TO THE MODERN PEOPLE MOVER TRACK.

Greektown Character Stella Hangs Her Laundry On A Fence In Front Of The Detroit Police Headquarters On Beaubien.

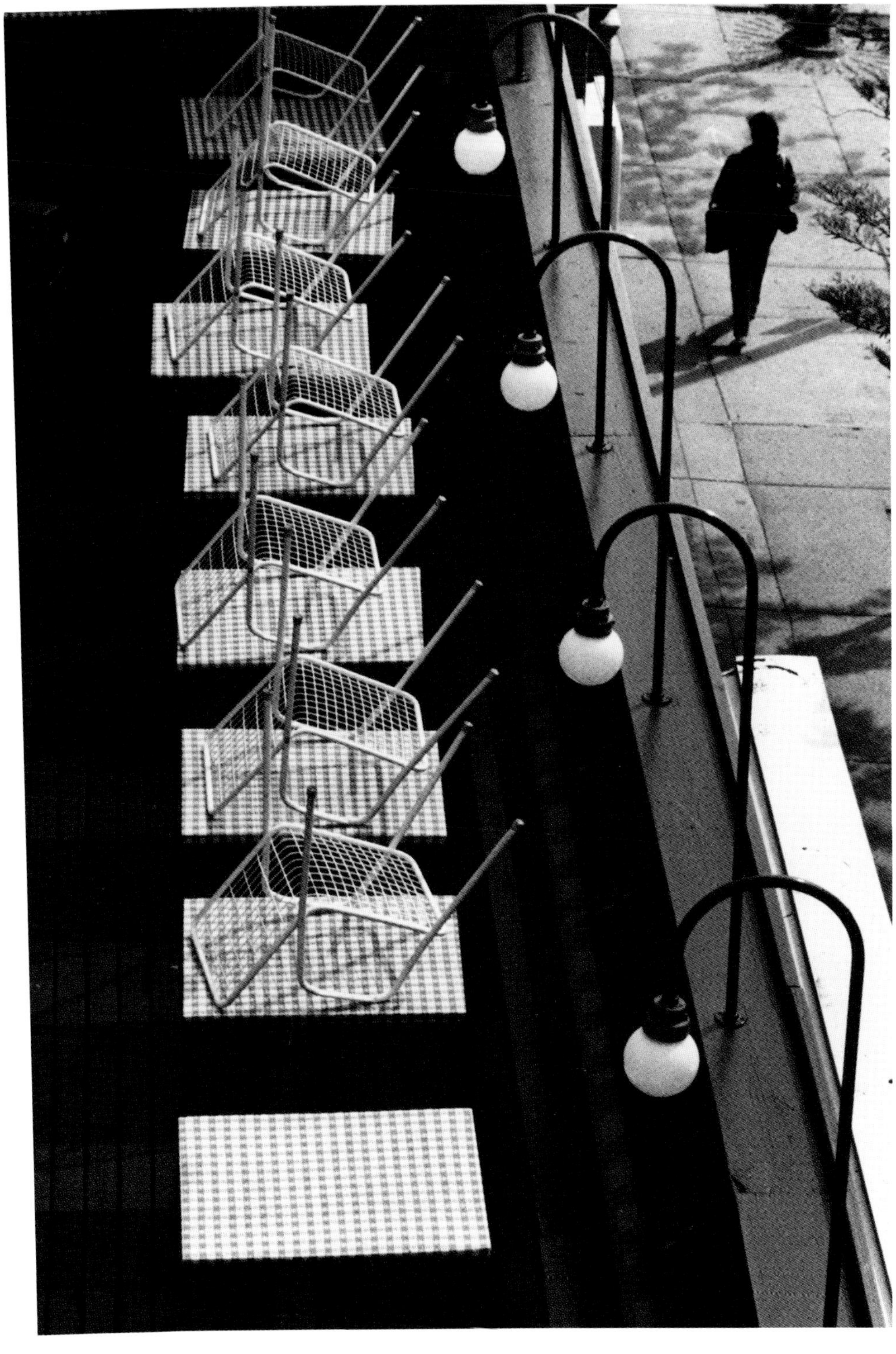

SUMMER FURNITURE AWAITS
WARMER DAYS ON THE TERRACE
OF GALLIGAN'S TAVERN
ON JEFFERSON.

A WORKER WALKS THE GUIDEWAY ALONG THE BANK OF THE DETROIT RIVER NEAR JOE LOUIS ARENA.

The Westin Hotel Tower Of The Renaissance Center And The Apartments Of The Millender Center Stand Side By Side.

A PEEPING-TOM VIEW OF A WORKER AT THE CITY-COUNTY BUILDING. THIS LATE AFTERNOON WAS RESERVED FOR READING THE PAPER.

ELECTION

A Downtown Worker With Softball Uniform And Suit Leaves Work And Heads To A Game.

A Motorcycle Officer Leaves Downtown Headquarters.

MADIS
PIZZA
FULL PIES
or by SLICE

THE AGING MARQUEE OF THE MADISON THEATRE ON GRAND CIRCUS PARK, WITH NOTHING TO TOUT.

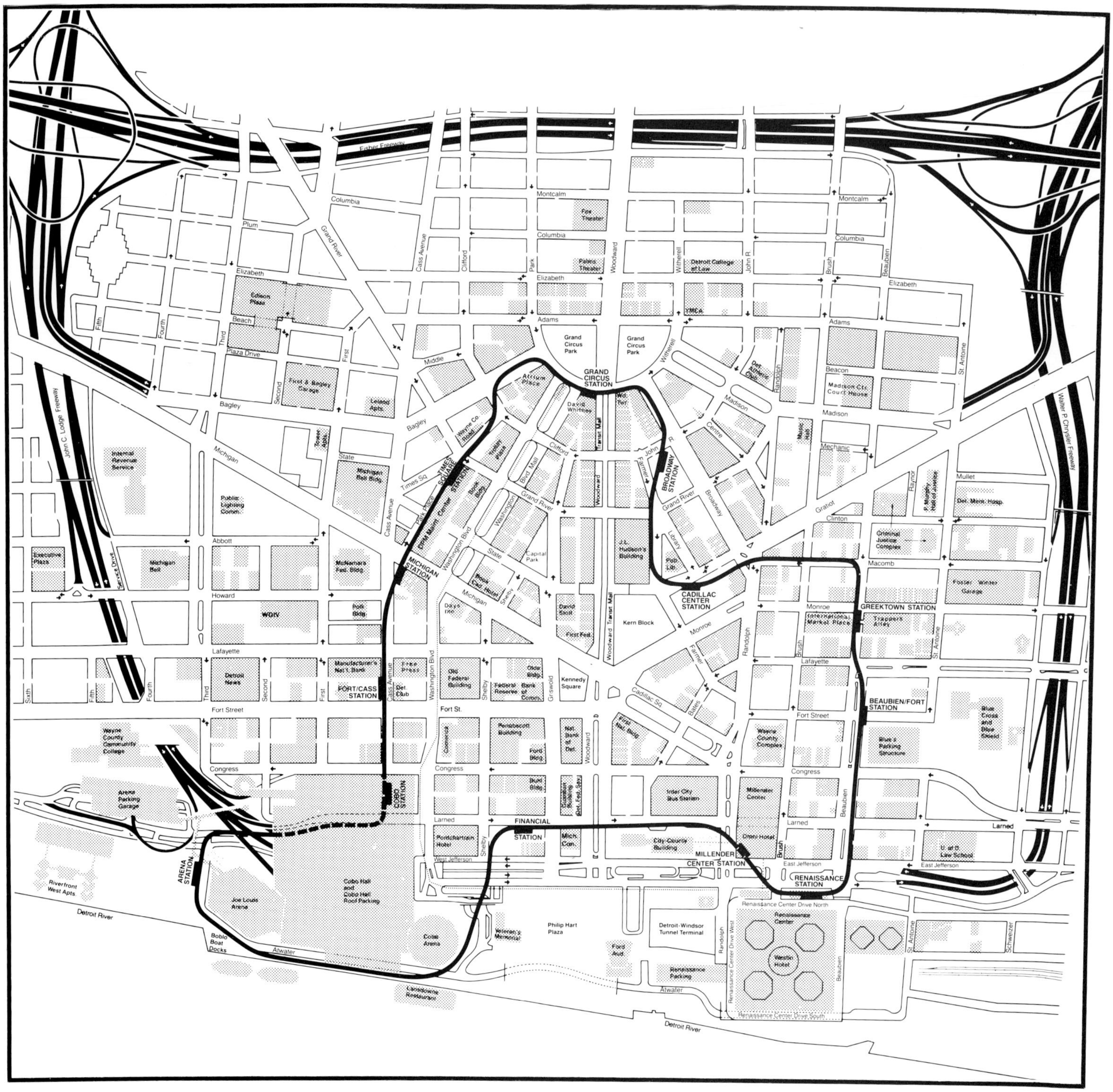

Fisher Freeway
Montcalm
Columbia
Plum
Fox Theater
Palms Theater
Detroit College of Law
Grand River
Cass Avenue
Clifford
Park
Woodward
Witherell
John R
Brush
Beaubien
Elizabeth
Edison Plaza
Beach
Fifth
Fourth
Third
Second
First
Plaza Drive
Adams
Grand Circus Park
YMCA
St. Antoine
First & Bagley Garage
Middle
Leland Apts.
Bagley
GRAND CIRCUS STATION
Atrium Place
David Whitney
Wd. Twr.
Det. Athletic Club
Randolph
Beacon
Madison Ctr. Court House
Madison
Wayne Co. Road
Trolley Plaza
Transit Mall
Farmer
Centre
Music Hall
Mechanic
John C. Lodge Freeway
Walter P. Chrysler Freeway
Internal Revenue Service
Michigan
State
Tower Apts.
Michigan Bell Bldg.
Times Sq.
TIMES SQUARE STATION
BROADWAY STATION
Broadway
Mullet
Raynor
Hall of Justice
Det. Mem. Hosp.
Public Lighting Comm.
Gratiot
Clinton
Criminal Justice Complex
Abbott
Executive Plaza
Michigan Bell
McNamara Fed. Bldg.
Service Drive
Washington Blvd
Capital Park
J.L. Hudson's Building
Library
Pub. Lib.
Macomb
Foster Winter Garage
MICHIGAN STATION
Howard
WDIV
David Stott
CADILLAC CENTER STATION
Monroe
GREEKTOWN STATION
International Market Place
Trappers Alley
Polk Bldg.
Days Inn
Kern Block
First Fed.
Woodward Transit Mall
Lafayette
Detroit News
Manufacturer's Nat'l. Bank
Free Press
Old Federal Building
Federal Reserve
Olde Bldg.
Kennedy Square
Griswold
Shelby
Cadillac Sq.
Bates
FORT/CASS STATION
Det. Club
Sixth
BEAUBIEN/FORT STATION
Fort Street
Fort St.
Wayne County Community College
Comerica
Penobscot Building
Ford Bldg.
Wayne County Complex
Blue Cross and Blue Shield
Congress
Arena Parking Garage
COBO STATION
Buhl Bldg.
Guardian Building
Det. Fed. Sav.
Inter City Bus Station
Millender Center
Larned
FINANCIAL STATION
Pontchartrain Hotel
Mich. Con.
City-County Building
Omni Hotel
MILLENDER CENTER STATION
U. of D. Law School
West Jefferson
East Jefferson
RENAISSANCE STATION
ARENA STATION
Riverfront West Apts.
Joe Louis Arena
Cobo Hall and Cobo Hall Roof Parking
Detroit River
Boblo Boat Docks
Atwater
Cobo Arena
Veteran's Memorial
Philip Hart Plaza
Ford Aud.
Detroit-Windsor Tunnel Terminal
Renaissance Center Drive North
Renaissance Center
Westin Hotel
Renaissance Center Drive West
Renaissance Parking
Renaissance Center Drive South
Schweizer
Lansdowne Restaurant